Ruach HaKodesh

The Holy Spirit
Just Who Is He?

By Loleen Denney
Tree of Life Ministries

Ruach HaKodesh
The Holy Spirit Just Who Is He?
by Loleen Denney

Printed in the United States of America

ISBN 978-1-60477-821-2

Unless otherwise indicated, Bible quotations are taken from The Amplified Bible. Copyright © 1965 by Zondervan Publishing House

Contact information:
Tree of Life Ministries
Loleen Denney
Box 1387
Pinedale, Wy. 82941
E-mail: mdenney@wyoming.com

www.xulonpress.com

TABLE OF CONTENTS

RUACH HAKODESH

Prelude

This book has evolved from writing a term paper. When it was suggested that I write my paper on the Holy Spirit, my first thought was "how controversial" it could be. I then became a bit apprehensive because of the different thoughts and camps of thought. I quickly started praying and fasting. The last thing I wanted was this paper to be my opinion and the first thing I wanted was for the Holy Spirit to totally lead me. I continued to pray, read, and research the bible, make notes, and pray some more.

The day that I sat down to write was pretty much like any ordinary day. I had procrastinated as long as I could and the time had come for me to put "pen to paper" so to speak. My continual prayer had been, "Holy Spirit what do You want to say. What do You want people to know about You?" As I began to type my thoughts were led to what would the paper look like if the Holy Spirit did in deed write it. I decided to allow the thoughts to have their way. I am so glad that I did. The two days that it took to write have become life changing for me and have changed how I perceived the Holy Spirit up to that point.

I have always had a close relationship with my Heavenly Father and my Friend and Savior Jesus. From the beginning of my Christian walk I have had many intimate moments and experiences with them. Unfortunately I found myself often confused over what people taught and what I perceived to be information about the Holy Spirit. I knew about being filled with Him. I knew how to pray effectively in the Spirit. I guess I just never considered Him as much of an individual as I did Father God and Jesus. I always went to them, but it rarely occurred to me to go to the Holy Spirit in the same intimate way.

The two days I wrote have forever changed that. I experienced Him as if over a cup of tea and He was telling a friend of His history. I now find myself with a new respect, hunger, and awareness of His presence. Just knowing that He is the very spiritual breath I breathe every day has awakened my soul in a new way. My spirit is more in tune with what He is saying, and that He is as much of an individual of the Godhead as my Heavenly Father or Jesus. After 30 years of good seasons and a lot of hard times in those seasons of walking with the Lord, I have found an awakening within me, a returning of my joy, my first love, and my excitement.

I have found that the Holy Spirit is most alive and vibrant when He is able to give someone a deeper, new revelation of Who Father God is, the depth of the work that Jesus accomplished when here on earth, and the eternal ramifications of Jesus' resurrection for people that accept Him and become believers. His most dynamic animation comes when He is allowed to freely lead believers into deeper understanding of Heavenly matters, the presence of the Lord, and especially things of the cross.

I have come to realize in more depth why the enemy of our souls has worked so hard to divide the Body of Christ over our belief systems about the Holy Spirit. The enemy KNOWS the power that will be unleashed against his kingdom when the believers quit fighting **over** the Holy Spirit and unite **in** the Holy Spirit. When our deepest desire becomes allowing the Holy Spirit free reign in our lives and church bodies, we will once again experience the character of the Holy Spirit revolutionizing the world for Jesus. We will once again experience the power of His presence and the wonders of His gifts fully operating and freely giving life to a dying world.

We MUST learn how to lean in lovingly, respectfully, and in total submission to the Holy Spirit. We MUST allow Him to freely be the air we breathe. We MUST allow His character and all it encompasses to become our character. We MUST allow Him to overshadow us, impregnate us with truth, and give birth to life through the Blood of Jesus. We are to be the carriers of His Glory to impart to anyone who is hungry for reality.

In His love
Loleen

DEDICATION

I dedicate this book to the team of intercessors that have prayed faithfully for Tree of Life Ministries, my family, and me for the last number of years. I also want to thank my husband, Mike, for encouraging me, allowing me freedom to travel, to minister, and praying for me. You haven't always understood me, but you have always stood beside me.

INTRODUCTION

If the Holy Spirit were to write this paper, what would He say? Would He question, "Who do people say I am? Why do they believe it? Is that really Who I am?" Would He defend Himself from the misconception and lies that seem to be prevalent in the Church? Would He explain His part of the Trinity Godhead, Elohim, (Jehovah, Adonai, and Ruach are Elohim). Would He in pride display His power to prove everyone's theory wrong? Just how would He describe who He is, what He does, His character and nature, where He manifests and in what form? If we care to listen attentively, He in His gentle meekness, will quietly without defense tell us truths of His history and of His who, what, where, and why.

THE BREATH OF GOD

"In the beginning…" How many times have you heard that phrase? You read in Gen. 1:1 that "in the beginning God created", and in John 1:1 "in the beginning was the Word" (Jesus). The church tends to forget that I the Holy Spirit was also "in the beginning moving, brooding, and hovering". Jehovah God was the thought behind creation. Adonai, Jesus was the vehicle of the Word spoken to create. I was the power source breathed from the midst of Elohim (the plurality of God). We each had our purpose and job to accomplish. We worked in unison creating perfection.

After We created a place for man to live and had provided for all of his needs, We set about creating him in Our image. As Elohim, (the embodiment of the Father, Son, and Holy Spirit), knelt down He worked so carefully, diligently forming, and fashioning every facet of this creation called man to commune with Him. Man's covering was the very presence of God and His glory surrounding him. When Elohim was finished He leaned over this man He called Adam and blew the Breath of Life into Our creation that caused Eternal Life to spring forth in Adam.

> *Then the Lord God formed man from the dust of the ground and breathed into his nostrils the breath or spirit of life, and man became a living being. (Gen. 2:7)x*
>
> *Gen. 2:7 Hebrew word used for Lord according to Strong's Exhaustive Concordance...3068 is Jehovah (endnote 1). The word used for God...Strong's Exhaustive Concordance Hebrew...430 is Elohim (endnote 2)*

For you see, Adam was **filled** with Me, the Holy Spirit, from his first breath. My name in Hebrew, Ruach HaKodesh, means spirit, wind, and breath. I am in the midst of Elohim. I am the Spirit of God, the very spirit breath of Elohim. Because I am breath and wind My substance is not as tangible, touchable, definable, or confinable as people would like. I suspect that has been the problem. Man wants to have a trophy he can display that reveals what he has caught. Unfortunately, in a three dimensional world invisible breath and wind do not display very well.

When Adam sinned and fell from grace he lost the right to be clothed in the glory of the presence of Elohim. He lost the right to walk and talk in the cool of the day with physical Adoni (his Lord). He lost the ability to be filled with Ruach, the spirit breath. This was Our original plan; every man or woman begotten of Adam and Eve would be clothed with Our presence, would be able to converse intimately with Us, and would be filled with the spirit breath of Us. Unfortunately, Adam sold those rights for mankind. Elohim's enemy, Satan, knew how powerful man would be. Satan was jealous of man being able to experience the fullness of Our Presence. That right Satan lost because of his pride.

So for thousands of years I could only come upon men or women who had willing hearts and hearing ears to hear Us and the courage to be used of Us. What Our enemy did not know was Our plan to purchase back everything Adam had sold through the redemptive blood of Adonai, Jesus the Savior. The timing was crucial. We had diligently worked through many to speak forth the prophetic words necessary to release the power needed to perform the miracles that would change the world and once again fill man/woman with the Spirit of Elohim.

CONCEPTION

J esus' mother Mary, what a heart she had. She so willingly surrendered herself to Elohim. She submitted herself to be used as the vessel to bring forth Adonai, the Word, Jesus. We knew that the Savior must be born of the Spirit. We knew He must carry the sinless blood of the Father. Even your scientists now recognize that the blood of the unborn child does not come from the mother and only takes place with the fertilization of the sperm of the father.

> *It is now definitely known that the blood which flows in an unborn babe's arteries and veins is not derived from the mother but is produced within the body of the foetus. Yet it is only after the sperm has entered the ovum and a foetus begins to develop that blood appears...The Chemistry of the Blood... endnote 3*

The foetal blood in the vessels of the chorionic villae AT NO TIME GAINS ACCESS TO THE MATERNAL BLOOD in the intervillous spaces, BEING SEPARATED FROM ONE ANOTHER by the double layer of chorionic epithelium...Practice of Obstetrics...endnote 4

When the circulation of the blood begins in the embryo, it remains separate and distinct from that of the mother. All food and waste material which are interchanged between the embryo and the mother must pass through the blood vessel walls from one circulation to the other...Nurse's Handbook of Obstetrics...endnote 5

The overshadowing of Mary by "The Breath of God" causing the conception of Jesus as the vehicle that carried the sinless blood of the Father to redeem mankind from sin was Our plan. Mary always had the right of choice to refuse, but she desired as a surrendered handmaiden of God to do Elohim's will.

And Mary said to the angel, How can this be, since I have no [intimacy with any man as a] husband? Then the angel said to her, the Holy Spirit will come upon you, and the power of the Most High will overshadow you [like a shining cloud]; and so the holy (pure, sinless) thing (Offspring) which shall be born of you will be called the Son of God...(Luke 1:34-35)

Then Mary said, Behold, I am the hand-maiden of the Lord; let it be done to me according to what you have said. And the angel left her... (Luke 1:38)

THE HOLY SPIRIT'S INFLUENCE IN JESUS

I taught Jesus as He grew. He learned well and spoke with great love and authority about His Father. The day that His cousin John baptized Him was monumental indeed...

In those days Jesus came from Nazareth of Galilee and was baptized by John in the Jordan. And when He came up out of the water, at once he [John] saw the heavens torn open and the [Holy] Spirit like a dove coming down[to enter] into Him and there came a voice out from within heaven, you are My Beloved Son; in You I am well pleased. Immediately the [Holy] Spirit [from within] drove Him out into the wilderness (desert). (Mark 1:9-12)

Elohim once again was able to blow Ruach, the breath of life, into man. I then took Jesus into the wilderness, a place of privacy, to finish preparing Him for the work and ministry that would in the end take His life. As Adonai He knew We were purchasing back all that Adam sold.

Jesus' character, because of His total surrender, was My character. He allowed Me to fill Him. I was able to move freely in, around, and through Him. All of My attributes were released in Him. Everything I am, He was...

But the fruit of the [Holy] Spirit [the work which His presence within accomplishes] is love, joy (gladness), peace, patience (an even temper, forbearance), kindness, goodness, (benevolence), faithfulness, gentleness (meekness, humility), self-control (self-restraint, continence). Against such there is no law [that can bring a charge]. (Gal. 5:22-23)

Jesus carried within Him all the power that Elohim intended for man to walk in. He walked in every manifestation of every gift that I had to release into mankind. He became the living example of those gifts, operating in them powerfully, unselfishly.

Now there are distinctive varieties and distributions of endowments (gifts, extraordinary powers distinguishing certain Christians, due to the power of divine grace operating in their souls by the Holy Spirit) and they vary, but the [Holy] Spirit remains the same, and there are distinctive varieties of service and ministration, but it is the same Lord[who is served]. And there are distinctive varieties of operation [of working to accomplish things], but it is the same God Who inspires and energizes them all in all. But to each one is given the manifestation of the [Holy] Spirit [the evidence, the spiritual illumination of the Spirit] for good and profit. To one is given in and through the [Holy] Spirit [the power to speak] a message of wisdom, and to another [the power to express] a word of knowledge and understanding according to the same [Holy] Spirit; To another the working of miracles, to another prophetic insight (the gift of interpreting the divine will and purpose; to another the ability to discern ad distinguish between [the utterances of true] spirits [and false ones], to another various kinds of [unknown] tongues, to another the ability to interpret [such] tongues. All these [gifts, achievements, abilities] are inspired and brought to pass by one and the same [Holy] Spirit, who apportions to each person individually [exactly] as He chooses... (1Cor. 12:4-11).

THE HOLY SPIRIT GIVEN TO MANKIND

After Jesus' death and resurrection Jesus appeared to His disciples confirming the important fact that He was indeed alive. Equally as important He prepared those disciples to receive Me. I spent that time in between His resurrection and Pentecost preparing their hearts. I taught them the importance of being in one accord. I placed within them an excitement that grew daily until the time had fully come for My manifestation.

> *And having said this, He breathed on them and said to them, Receive the Holy Spirit! ... (John 20:22)*
>
> *But you shall receive power (ability, efficiency, and might) when the Holy Spirit has come upon you, and you shall be My witnesses in Jerusalem and all Judea and Samaria and*

to the ends (the very bounds) of the earth...
(Acts 1:8)

Pentecost, ah Pentecost, was the day I looked forward to since the man Adam sinned. I would once again be able to fill mankind with the Breath of God. The very presence of Elohim would be free to manifest with the tongues of His glory clothing man. Elohim once again blew the wind of His Presence into man filling him with life. I can still hear the inhale of Elohim as He filled His lungs to the fullest before He blew into that upper room. The sound from heaven shook everything. Each person there became filled to the fullest with My presence in them. It was My day of freedom. I became the air they breathed once again.

> *And when the day of Pentecost had fully come, they were all assembled together in one place, When suddenly there came a sound from heaven like the rushing of a violent tempest blast, and it filled the whole house in which they were sitting. And there appeared to them tongues resembling fire, which were separated and distributed and which settled on each one of them. And they were all filled (diffused throughout their souls) with the Holy Spirit and began to speak in other (different, foreign) languages (tongues), as the Spirit kept giving them clear and loud expression [in each tongue in appropriate words]... (Acts 2:1-4)*

The joy that was released even made some of the people present think that these in the upper room had been drinking. The accusation that they were drunk with sweet wine was partially true. They were drunk with the spiritual sweetness of Elohim's breath. They were experiencing My joy of being allowed to be free in mankind once again. Love diffused every part of their being. I must admit self-control was a little hard that day for My joy was so pervasive. These disciples who had been so fearful just a few days ago now exhibited boldness contrary to their character. They boldly exclaimed Elohim's plan. Peter, who had just a little over a month before denied Jesus, now with eloquence and revelation explained concisely how anyone who desired to believe in Jesus would have salvation and could be filled with Me. The people around them could plainly see that these disciples were not learned men. The surprise was they spoke like learned men because of the influence of the "Breath of God" that had been released in them. That day I was not only released in them, but I was released to fill anyone who believed for as many generations as would exist before the Second Coming of Adonai.

And Peter answered them, Repent (change your views and purpose to accept the will of God in your inner selves instead of rejecting it) and be baptized, every one of you, in the name of Jesus Christ for the forgiveness of and release from your sins; and you shall receive the gift of the Holy Spirit. For the promise [of the Holy Spirit] is to and for you and your children, and to and for all that are far away, [even] to and for as many as the Lord our God invites and bids to come to Himself...(Acts 2:38-39)

BELIEVERS LED OF THE HOLY SPIRIT

The days that followed were exciting. The disciples didn't fully understand what had happened to them. They just knew that they were different and contained a faith that they did not have before. Their prayers were answered even before they could utter them. They delighted in spending time fellowshipping with each other, encouraging each other, and learning from Me about Adonai, their Lord. My purpose was to lead them into all Truth. Give them wisdom, knowledge, and revelation of their Messiah. I gave them understanding of Who their Father God truly was, why Jesus was sent, and how to walk powerfully with My anointing in them. Because of their submission and willingness, many were brought into Eternal Life through salvation by the pure Blood of Jesus. The number of believers increased daily. They learned to walk in the same character and power as their Jesus had. They allowed their character to be changed into My character because they believed and submitted to My leading in their lives.

Unfortunately there were people that did not have the right motives, were unscrupulous in their hearts, and allowed that deceiver, Satan, to pollute them. Some even thought that they could purchase Me with their gold as if I were something they could control. Their motives were pride, power, manipulation, and control over others. They did not understand that I was a gift, a free gift to those that believe. Some who had been filled with Me even lost their lives when I had to remove myself from them because of their lies, deceit, and blaspheme.

But there was a man named Simon, who had formerly practiced magic arts in the city to the utter amazement of the Samaritan nation, claiming that he himself was an extraordinary and distinguished person....(Acts 8:9) then [the apostles] laid their hands on them one by one, and they received the Holy Spirit. However, when Simon saw that the [Holy] Spirit was imparted through the laying on of the apostles' hands, he brought money and offered it to them, Saying, Grant me also this power and authority, in order that anyone on whom I place my hands may receive the Holy Spirit. But Peter said to him, Destruction overtake your money and you, because you imagined you could obtain the [free] gift of God with money!... (Acts 8:17-20)

But a certain man named Ananias with his wife Sapphira sold a piece of property,... (Acts 5:1) Then Peter said to her, How could you two have agreed and conspired together to try to deceive the Spirit of the Lord? Listen! The feet of those who have buried your husband are at the door, and they will carry you out [also]... (Acts 5:9)

THE HOLY SPIRIT'S INFLUENCE IN PAUL

At times it was difficult to change the believers' thinking because of the religiousness of their belief system. The Pharisees had taught many untruths about the power, presence, and heart of Elohim. Paul was a powerful Pharisee with much ambition. He truly thought that he was doing the work his God required of him. He thought that he was defending Elohim whom he greatly loved. When Jesus dramatically presented Himself to Paul on the road to Damascus, Paul realized that he had been wrong. He allowed Me to diligently unravel the lies from the Truth. Even to this current day, the enemy has intertwined religion with reality. Satan skillfully has taught lies that seem as the truth. He counts on the self nature of mankind to rule supreme. He has been somewhat successful, but there are multitudes of people who are willingly laying down their lives both spiritually and physically in total submission to their Adonai. Paul is but an example of how a submitted heart to Me that is willing to learn of the Messiah and His purpose of salvation can affect the world.

Paul spent time studying, praying, asking Me questions. He became such a Truth seeker. His knowledge of Torah and the prophets became alive to him when he was able to understand Jesus' fulfillment of all of the scriptures. What a student of understanding he became. He allowed Me to continually give him revelation after revelation of Us. He surrendered everything that at one time had been important to him enabling him to teach and write so that the believers that were being added daily could in simplicity understand what he understood. It was not an easy life he chose, but a rewarding one as he saw Truth and Life spring alive in the hearts of the Messiah followers.

THE FRUIT AND GIFTS OF THE HOLY SPIRIT

Paul so grasped the understanding of My character, he even called it My fruit. What a student of human nature he was. He understood the nature that Satan had sown into man was contrary to the nature of Elohim. He did not hold back any words of description when he taught the difference between the enemy's fruit of influence and My fruit of influence. He not only taught them, but he encouraged them into the understanding that changing their sinful nature to a Godly nature was possible and attainable through submission to Me.

Satan especially didn't like Paul teaching on the gifts that I had released into the body of believers. This enemy of your souls has caused such confusion, division, and distrust among the church body. Satan's line of defense if he couldn't stop someone from receiving salvation through Jesus' blood was to make them dull of hearing. If that didn't work then he caused confusion about the gifts and if they were for everybody. The current lie he has fostered has to do with the gifts being for this day and age. My gifts are as operable and powerful today as they were 2000 years ago. They have not passed away, the perfection has not come. That time is at the end of the age. The argument of Jesus being the perfection is a mixture of truth and untruth. Jesus is, was, and will always be perfection but when Paul was writing in Corinthians about the perfection passing away I had him looking forward to the returning of the King of Kings, the closing of the age and the coming of the New Jerusalem. Paul understood while John saw.

Love never fails [never fades out or becomes obsolete or comes to an end]. As for prophecy (the gift of interpreting the divine will and purpose), it will be fulfilled and pass away; as for tongues, they will be destroyed and cease; as for knowledge, it will pass away [it will lose its value and be superseded by truth]. For our knowledge is fragmentary (incomplete and imperfect), and our prophecy (our teaching) is fragmentary (incomplete and imperfect). But when the complete and perfect (total) comes, the incomplete and imperfect will vanish away (become antiquated, void, and superseded)... (1Cor. 13:8-10)

Then I saw a new sky (heaven) and a new earth, for the former sky and the former earth had passed away (vanished), and there no longer existed any sea. And I saw the holy city, the new Jerusalem, descending out of heaven from God, all arrayed like a bride beautified and adorned for her husband; Then I heard a mighty voice from the throne and I perceived its distinct words, saying, See! The abode of God is with men, and He will live (encamp, tent) among them; and they shall be His people, and God shall personally be with them and be their God. God will wipe away every tear from their eyes; and death shall be no more, neither shall there be anguish (sorrow and mourning) nor grief nor pain any more, for the old conditions and the former order of things have passed away. And He Who is seated on the throne said, See! I make all things new. Also He said, Record this, for these sayings are faithful (accurate, incorruptible, and trustworthy) and true (genuine)... (Rev. 21:1-5)

TONGUES...TO SPEAK OR NOT TO SPEAK

Paul learned and taught the secret of spending time with Me. The importance of his allowing Me to guide his prayers. He allowed Me to pray through him, to pray the things that were on Elohim's heart. He learned the power of praying in the Holy Spirit. The enemy of your souls has taken this gift and twisted and turned it. He has caused much division, hurt, and misconception. He has caused his fruit of pride to enter to the heart of man keeping man from surrendering to Me and allowing Me to edify him, strengthen him, lead and guide him. Satan has lied, caused much pride and fear, and entangled with confusion My gift of tongues and interpretation with My edifying ability to pray powerfully through man. I know that man knows only partially what is on his Father's heart. I, the searcher of the heart, know how to pray effectively with power. If man would but submit, I would be better able to show him the secret things of the Father, pray more effectively through him about his troubles, and give him more easily the solutions that are needed to live in this corrupt world. Praying with My help builds up his spiritual strength, gives insight, and encourages him to keep going when he thinks he cannot go any farther. I am the groaning of the heart expressed privately when no man's words can fill the need. The gift of tongues and interpretation speaks to man, praying in the spirit prayer language is the communication between man and his Father. It is not for a select few, but is for all believers.

> *For one who speaks in an[unknown] tongue speaks not to men but to God, for no one understands or catches his meaning, because in the [Holy] Spirit he utters secret truths and hidden things [not obvious to the understanding]. (1Cor. 14:2)*
>
> *He who speaks in a [strange] tongue edifies and improves himself, but he who prophesies [interpreting the divine will and purpose and teaching with inspiration] edifies and improves the church and promotes growth [in Christian wisdom, piety, holiness, and happiness]...(1Cor. 14:4)*
>
> *For if I pray in an [unknown] tongue, my spirit [by the Holy Spirit within me] prays, but my mind is unproductive [it bears no fruit and helps nobody]. Then what am I to do? I will pray with my spirit [by the Holy Spirit that is within me], but I will also pray [intel-*

*ligently] with my mind and understanding;
I will sing with my spirit [by the Holy spirit
that is within me], but I will sing [intelli-
gently] with my mind and understanding also.
Otherwise, if you bless and render thanks
with [your] spirit [thoroughly aroused by the
Holy Spirit], how can anyone in the position
of an outsider or he who is not gifted with
[interpreting of unknown] tongues, say the
Amen to your thanksgiving, since he does
not know what you are saying?...(1Cor. 14:
14-16)*

*I thank God that I speak in [strange]
tongue (language) more than any of you or all
of you put together; Nevertheless, in public
worship, I would rather say five words with
my understanding and intelligently in order
to instruct others, than ten thousand words
in a [strange] tongue (language)...(1Cor.
14:18-19)*

You see, Paul understood and taught the difference between My private tongue and My public
tongue. He understood that the private prayer tongue
was for everyone who was a believer. He also understood that the public tongue needed interpretation so
that the unbeliever would understand what was being
said and become a believer. Unfortunately the very
thing that was designed to strengthen and unify the
body individually and collectively has been used of
the enemy to cause much division. If he can't get
people to walk in his fear concerning it, then he sows

much pride in the belief that it is a special private endowment only meant for a few. The private questions that the body must ask themselves are: what is their belief, why do they have it, is it the truth, and why are they afraid to ask Me the truth.

TOTAL SURRENDER

Paul and the disciples learned that no matter what came their way, eternal life was their goal and prize. They allowed Me to manifest in My many faceted way in them. They allowed Me to comfort them, fill them with joy knowing that their surrender placed Elohim in control, and I was able to surround them with peace. They willing allowed Me to lead them to the fulfillment of their destiny. What could man do to them when total surrender to Elohim and Eternal Life awaited them. Being in Our Presence was more desirable than any temporary situation man could force them into. That is why Stephen and all believers down through the ages have been able to boldly stand in the presence of the religious people. They know the tangible hope in which they believe. They know that this physical life is but a temporary moment in eternity. They know that to be absent from this flesh and blood body is to be present with Elohim for all time. Even as they were killing Stephen, he was able to forgive because he saw the hope of his salvation. The hope, the hope is the strength that I impart to all who surrender by way of the Blood of Adoni, their personal Lord.

> *Now upon hearing these things, they [the Jews] were cut to the heart and infuriated, and they ground their teeth against [Stephen]. But he, full of the Holy Spirit and controlled by Him, gazed into heaven and saw the glory (the splendor and majesty) of God, and Jesus standing at God's right hand; and he said, Look! I see the heavens opened, and the Son of man standing at God's right hand!... (Acts 7:54-56)*
>
> *And while they were stoning Stephen, he prayed, Lord Jesus, receive and accept and welcome my spirit! And falling on his knees, he cried out loudly, Lord, fix not this sin upon them [lay it not to their charge]! And when he had said this he fell asleep [in death]... (Acts 7:59-60)*

CONCLUSION

I, Ruach HaKodesh, was in the beginning of creation, I am present in the NOW, and I will be through eternity. I am the same, have been the same, and will always be the same. I never change. I lead all men that will be led into all truth about Elohim. We, Elohim, (the Father, the Son, and the Spirit) are One in Our purpose for mankind, in Our manifestation to mankind, and in Our destiny of mankind. I teach of the Father and the Son. None can come to the Father by the blood of the Messiah, His Son, unless I first draw them. My strength of manifestation in this human world rests on the prayers of the saints that have surrendered to belief in their Savior, Jesus. The more they pray the more I am free to manifest. The more individual surrendering done the more powerful the collective move I am free to do. I am the Breath of Life given to each who believe. It is man's choice as to how full of that breath he wants to be. It is man's choice how much of that breath is

47

breathed into a dying world. I stand ready…moving, brooding, hovering.

20 THOUGHTS TO PONDER

1. When Elohim blew breath into Adam's nostrils He not only blew physical air but transferred a portion of Ruach HaKodesh to Adam's being. It caused him to not only be filled with oxygen but also the Holy Spirit from his first breath.
   Genesis 2:7 I Corinthians 15:45-49

2. The Glory of God is a tangible touchable substance that can encompass and cover. Sin and unbelief will cause it to dissipate like sunlight on fog.
   Matthew 17:1-8 II Peter 1:16-18

3. Adam sold our clothing, conversation, and 'breathing' rights to the enemy (Lucifer/Satan) of our souls.
   Genesis 3

4. The need for purity of the sacrifice *FOR* mankind necessitated the need for the impregnation of

Mary to be from a "father" whose blood had not been contaminated *BY* mankind.

Luke 1:27-35

5. Father God *NEVER* over rules man's right of choice.

Deuteronomy 30:19 Joshua 24:15 Psalms 25:12

6. Elohim encouraged Jesus before He took him to a place of privacy to finish His preparation for ministry by confirming His love and pleasure in him. Elohim does the same with us.

Matthew 3:16-4:1

7. The Fruit of the Spirit is not a by-product of the Holy Spirit. The Fruit is WHO He is and the attributes ARE His personality.

Galatians 5:22-25

8. The Gifts of the Holy Spirit are what He does. They are a manifestation of His presence and character.

I Corinthians 12:1-11

9. Jesus released the Holy Spirit within Him to the disciples to prepare them, to teach them how to be in one accord, and to have the expectation of a new manifestation of power when He blew on them.

John 20:21-22

10. Pentecost was the final step in purchasing back our clothing, conversation, and 'breathing' rights that Adam had sold. Mankind was once again able to be CREATION COMPLETE. He was clothed with the tongues of Glory, filled with

Ruach's breath of life, and given the ability to talk intimately with Elohim once again.
Acts 2:1-4

11. The Holy Spirit never points to Himself. He always focuses on Father God and directs mankind to Jesus.
John 16:7-15 I Corinthians 2:7-16

12. We must examine the motives of our hearts when it comes to wanting the Holy Spirit's manifestations to flow through us and not allow our hearts to deceive us.
I John 3:18-24

13. The lies of religion will blind us to the truth of reality. Only the Holy Spirit can separate religion and reality leaving truthful insight behind in the eyes of the heart.
Acts 9:1-22 I Corinthians 12:3

14. Praying in the tongues prayer language of Ruach…the Holy Spirit…is equivalent to taking a deep lung full of air to counter act a smothered sensation.
John 20:22 Acts 2:1-4

15. Praying in tongues is our choice of submission. Pride will keep us in control and not surrendered.
Mark 16:17 Acts 19:1-6 I Corinthians 14:15

16. Tunnel vision causes us to focus on the here and now instead of forever future. We need eyes to see how small now is in comparison to eternity and learn to live in a larger field of vision.
Ecclesiastes 12:1-8 Mark 10:29-31 Isaiah 57:15-21

17. Here and now equals death. Eternity equals true life.
    I John 5:10-13

18. Interesting how Elohim has purposely limited His movement in the life of mankind to the surrendered prayers of believers in Jesus the true Messiah and Lord of man.
    Philippians 4:6-7 I Peter 3:12 I John 5:14-15

19. On the other hand it is equally interesting how Satan depends on the lack of prayer of true believers to further his agenda and how the prayers of unbelievers of Jesus increase the enemy of our soul's influence in the world of mankind.
    Matthew 17:16-21 I Peter 3:7

20. How much am I willing to pray to enlarge the limits of Elohim's movement in mankind?
    James 5:16

PRAYER

Holy Spirit, I ask that You lead me into ALL wisdom, truth, knowledge, and reality of my Father God and my Lord Jesus. Teach me the truth about Them. Teach me the truth about You. Teach me how to listen, be sensitive, and understand. Give me a desire to know the truth. Where I have believed a lie about the Godhead, purge it from me. Forgive me where I have grieved You as You were trying to lead and teach me. Forgive me when I have ignored what You have tried to cleanse from my heart. I desire to be filled with You, to be led of You, and to be taught by You. Forgive me when I have allowed myself to be afraid of You, of not wanting to submit to You. Cleanse out all the lies that the enemy of my soul and religion have taught me. I want only the reality of TRUTH to abide in me.

Fill me Holy Spirit. Infuse every fiber of my physical and spiritual being with Your presence.

Release in me the desire and ability to pray in the spirit. Teach me to pray effectively and powerfully in my prayer language, the language between man and his Father. Teach me to pray forth life, truth, and the mysteries of the Kingdom of God into my life and the life of the Church. Teach me to walk with You humbly in total submission to my Father's will for my life. Lead me into all truth and revelation about Jesus, His shed blood, and the love He has for me that led to His sacrifice. Lead me to the heart of my Father and to the depth of the understanding of the cross and what Jesus purchased. Lead me into the full understanding of the Godhead ... Elohim (Father-Jehovah God, Jesus-Adoni the Son, and the Holy Spirit-Ruach HaKodesh). Amen.

ENDNOTES

x. The Amplified Version will be used throughout this paper.

1. James Strong, S.T.D., LL.D., Strong's Exhaustive Concordance Of The Bible (MacDonald Publishing Company, McLean, Virginia 22102)
2. James Strong, S.T.D., LL.D., Strong's Exhaustive Concordance Of The Bible (MacDonald Publishing Company, McLean, Virginia 22102)
3. M. R. DeHaan, M.D., The Chemistry Of The Blood, Zondervan Publishing House, Grand Rapids, Michigan 49530
4. M. R. DeHaan, M.D., The Chemistry Of The Blood, Zondervan Publishing House, Grand Rapids, Michigan 49530 ...Quoted page 32 from Williams' Practice of Obstetrics, Third Edition, page 133
5. M. R. DeHaan, M.D., The Chemistry Of The Blood, Zondervan Publishing House, Grand Rapids, Michigan 49530 ...Quoted page 32 from

Louise Zabriskie, R.N., <u>Nurse's Handbook of Obstetrics,</u> Fifth Edition, page 75

Printed in the United States
115427LV00001B/253-414/P

9 781604 778212